COOKING LESSONS

Nina Romano

Cooking Lessons
By Nina Romano
Book Copyright © 2007 Nina Romano
Library of Congress Control Number: 2007922474

ISBN: 978-0-9676748-7-2
Printed in the United States of America
First Edition

Published by Rock Press, Inc.
4611 South University Drive #450
Davie, FL 33328 USA
www.Rock-Press.com

Direct inquiries and/or orders to the above address.

Designed by Melissa Macy.

ACKNOWLEDGMENTS

Grazie mille! to my husband, Felipe Romano, without whom there is no poetry.

I would like to extend sincere thanks to Tracey Broussard for generously affording me the opportunity of publishing these poems in a collection.

Special thanks to the many people who have encouraged me along the poetry pathway, and have read or critiqued my work: Campbell McGrath, John Dufresne, Denise Duhamel, Michael Hettich, JimDaniels, Cathy Bowman, Lynne Barrett, Cindy Chinelly, Jesse Millner, Rita Quinton, Mona Birch, Elaine Winer, Nico Romano, Phil De Simone, Marianne Haycook, Joan Waldman, Marni Graff, Lauren Small, Melissa Westemeier, Mariana Damon, Debra Wooley, Liang Guo, Alex Francischine, Lissette Mendez, Marie Lovas, Kathy Cappy, Haya Pomrenze, Jane Brownley, Cathy Anthony, the world's greatest librarian, and in loving memory of Millicent-Pelle Rynning, looking down from her celestial perch.

Grateful acknowledgement is made to the editors of the following publications, where these poems first appeared, some in different form:

Grain: "Luciana Vergara-Caffarelli's Recipe for: *Pasta ai Petali di Rosa*," "*Soriano nel Cimino* With Clemente That Sunday Playing Bridge With Mice"

Gulf Stream Magazine: "Recipe for *Buttariga*"

Roadspoetry: "The Deer Slayer," "Cruising," "Crucifixion of Garlic"

The Chrysalis Reader: "Bread"

Vox: "Tongues" and "Ave Maria" and the short story "The Deer Slayer," which contains part of the poem of the same name.

Voices in Italian Americana: "The Hazel Nut," "*Sardegna Ghazal*," and "Frying Zucchini"

Whiskey Island Magazine: "Buying Bread: the Art of Cementing International Relations"

Irrepressible Appetites: "Recipe for *Buttariga*," "The Hazel Nut," "Luciana Vergara Caffarelli's Recipe for *Pasta ai Petali di Rosa*"

COOKING LESSONS

Rock
Press

FOR YOU, MA

TABLE OF CONTENTS

I

COOKING LESSONS

COOKING LESSONS

The autumn when I was eleven, I began to cook.
Mamma was doing a charity luncheon for love
of the cloistered community where I got lessons
in the three R's and life, like how to steel
myself for the "onslaught" of problems life can dish
out, and how to "extricate" myself from hot water

when need arose. Mamma called to say boil water—
on her way, running late, so I'd have to cook
sauce for pasta. "First, set the table with everyday dishes,
your father'll make it home before I do, love,
so heat oil and garlic in a pot of stainless steel."
On the phone is where I got that lesson.

As if the worry of her lateness would lessen,
she called me back to say, "Careful with boiling water!
You've seen me prepare this dish—
I put the ingredients in terracotta to cook.
You can't mess up because food is love,
so if you can't find the pot of steel—"

"Not to worry, Mamma, the truth is I like to steal
recipes from you and Grandma. I've even had a lesson
or two from Auntie Gert who always says the love
is in the seasonings that make mouths water,
and it's simple enough to learn to cook,
if you watch. You can learn that creating a dish

is a snatch. *La* Gert also said, 'Remember when you dish
out any food, make it joyous, and never admit to steal-
ing others' menus. Just say you're a natural cook,
or possibly you could own up to having had one lesson
from your sweet old auntie—me.' " So as the pasta water
bubbled that fall eve, I daydreamed how someday I'd love

to write the Great Italo-American Novel of Love
and Food. I opened cans of tomatoes, put them in a dish;
squashed them into pulp, then rinsed my hands with water.
Tomatoes simmering, Dad arrived starved. About to steal
a taste of sauce upon a hunk of Italian bread, to lessen,
he said, the need for a king's taster, he kissed me, the cook.

Later Dad pinched Mamma's fanny as she washed dish-
es and soapy water swirled down the steel drain:
love and cooking lessons for a mini-kitchen wife.

BREAD

Before dawn Nico and I stood in line in the one general store
on the island of Ist. Roll call of the longest list of Slavic

names I've ever heard was ticked-off. When all had bread rations
tucked under arm, then we—sojourners—could buy if any remained.

One day when there was not a single scrap, not a loaf left,
an old man with two sold us one of his, patting Nico's cheek.

Weeks later at Korkula, we saw a fat lady sing in her window;
she hushed, and with puffed red, spidery cheeks, smiled at Nico.

I admired her basil plants on the sill behind wrought iron
freshly painted, so she picked and handed me a bunch.

Sunday everything's closed on the island hometown of Marco Polo.
I spoke to her in Sign—not a simple task with my baby in tow,

so I pointed to his ribs, touched his mouth, rubbed his belly,
cupped my hands, drawing them apart quick, quick—

the international sign for bread. She sent me to a nearby bar
and there an angel dressed in sailor suit spoke Italian

to me. The sailor's Slavic, almost good as my Sign,
convinced the owner to give me yesterday's

fragrant-wood-burning-stone-oven-baked-bread.
Zero dinars, zip dollars, zap lire. *"Regalo. Per favore."*

We shook hands. I thanked him for the gift. He tousled Nico's
hair; we waved, passing through the lintel of an ancient door.

FRYING ZUCCHINI

Green rounds sizzle in oil and it skitters. I stain my blouse
and shorts, recall Mom pouring noodle soup on my banana

curls when I refused to eat. I'd defied authority;
now despise the phantom

who stares back at me from the glass bottom casserole.
While arranging a batch of hot zucchini, I burn my fingers,

searing them with memories of what could've been.
Knife in hand, squash slicing, my mind skyrockets;

my heart palpitates a new rhythm at the thought of what I may
become tomorrow if I fry something larger like eggplants.

THE HAZEL NUT

round like me,
pointy at the top
like Clemente's ideas
of other universes,
scattered here and there
on a dwarfed tree of fall bounty—
this one plunked in between persimmons.
I cull a nut, winnow and bounce another
as a picker would, weighing fullness.
I crack the shell and crunch the core.
The sun-tongued firelight smokes and curlicues
acrid snakes above burning leaves.
It's autumn now in Soriano nel Cimino.
Who climbs our rooted hazel tree
now that you, friend,
are gone and I am
left remembering?

RECIPE FOR *BUTTARIGA*

From an exemplary female *muggine* better known as *cefalo*,
that has reached a certain dimension,
denoting its ovarian maturity,
remove, with a great deal of courtesy, the double ovary pack,
evading cuts in delicate membranes
leaving attached to the eggs
the harder part encasing the summit.

Cover both sides with fine salt, dry them,
place these on a cutting board of optimum wood—
aged for cutting. Cover caviar
with another board, laying on a heavy stone,
a 5 kilo rock, a grainy granite for weight and porosity.
Never compromise ends by too much squash or cleaver batting.
Leave for 2 or 3 days until the eggs reach
a 2 centimeter thinness, a length of 15.

The delicacy must dry in an ambient dwelling—
a room free of ocean salinity and night humidity.
The eggs are ready, achieving amber's transparency, colored *rosa cupo*.
Herein lies the difficulty—conserving *buttariga*.
Cloak entirely with wax hotter than a melting candle.

Later cut into thin slices with oil and lemon,
or grated to the fineness of Porto Rotondo sand,
let sift through fingers onto steamy *pasta* or *riso*.

A little hint—when no *cefalo* is available
a good-sized tuna,
possessing personality,
will suffice.

LUCIANA VERGARA-CAFFARELLI'S RECIPE

FOR: *PASTA AI PETALI DI ROSA*

We plucked pink, yellow, sometimes pearly whites, but never red
rose petals from unfumigated healthy bushes—true beauties,
a vision of herself in her Via Prisciano garden
where Nico and Carletto used to mud and wagon all around.

Pasta bleeds if reds are used, unbecoming *sanguine* like congealed
friendship. Vodka, cream and butter teased and blended in a perfect
marriage, then added to a dollop, mind, not a drop more of *pomodori*—
enhanced by *Parmigiano Reggiano*—a smidgen to amalgamate the whole

serving of *piccole penne rigate*—we wouldn't want to overpower ...
Overpower, overpowered me, pushed me over her terrace wall
where I fell to familiarity in front of Toragrossa's Funeral Parlor near
the Bay Eighth exit off the Southern State where there are plane trees,

horse chestnuts, maples and magnolias that put to shame any vestal
virgin palm, (fronds and all) bathed by powdery Prisciano dusk.
But what about a daring break-in through life's rear entrance?
Street level windows of access. Rain barrel. Cellar door.

Inside—a beast whose breath has gargled gardenias,
swallowed daffodils to the relenting rhythm of Cranberries.
Strawberry Fields Forever. Pre-Raphaelite. Arched columns.
Cushioned by white velvet, chic, we eat flowers for *eleganza*.

Which link is higher or lower in God's Chain?
Who will sit at the right hand? Angel, alive, I, least of all,
expected that Paradise or this detached *inferno* of your making.
Is living to dine, to feast, to sup, to eat,

to wine or is it to dive, to climb, to listen or to make love—
most vital of all our earthly acts? Or is it to be overcome,
overpowered, overwhelmed by this cucumber smell
as the rattlesnake strikes Luciana?

WILD GRAPES IN UNTENDED FIELD

(AFTER YUSEF KOMUNYAKAA)

Nico's fingertips brush-stroked
blue-black bright, almost enameled
like his mother's plum nailpolish,
or rouged the tawny sun-blush of her cheeks,

yanked tender *grappolo d'uva fragola*
towards sloping summer days where
they hung heavily inclining toward earth
& filled his hands with bunches to eat, sparing

others for a basket, while dreaming San Felice
sunfilled terrace mornings, *crostata di marmellata d'uva*—
a lattice crust, interwoven like love & guidance;
craved and carved into, honeyed spatula dripping.

Our goal-keeping dog Napoleon
attended Nico & neighbor children,
who, truant from labor, snuck off to La Cona's
tree-lined junction to peddle harvested fruit

destined for my jam pots and pies—money deposited later
in bar-front soccer machines—*cinquecento lire* to locals,
the mini-vagabonds bargained away my wild grapes.
Vacationing tourists glimpsed rat-pack palms,

moist with greed, thrust beneath their noses;
the two-bit tidbits testing outrageous trade waters—
tongue-tips unfamiliar with English, but accompanied
by hijacking smiles: "Pleeeze, one *dollaro.*"

ROASTED PEPPERS

The red skins sticky on my fingers as I pull and stretch and coax the seeds off the insides, and now there's something I want to do—wash my hands of the gooey glop, but I know I can't because my mother-in-law taught me how to peel these suckers, saying, never wash your hands with water—only pat them dry with paper towels else you'll ruin all your work. I continue, the sweet perfume of warm roasted peppers assails my nostrils so I'm transported back in time to Rome and her kitchen, paint peeling, wind blowing through the slats of the *serrande* shutters from the tiny terrace.

And now I know for sure we never die till the last person we know dies, for just as I am remembering her, so someone else I teach will remember me when I'm gone—even if it's just on a 3 X 5 recipe card. So I'll live on in their memory just as I swear she breathes and turns and laughs and tells me how much a mess roasted peppers make in her pristine, cracked porcelain sink.

As I peel and stack the peppers into an earthen glazed pot filled with green-gold Colavita Extra Virgin Olive Oil, speckled with pure white garlic cloves, I watch my son, as he counts out quarters from his savings bank with two Dutch children kissing on what looks like an old whiskey jug when hootch was illegal during Prohibition—my mother, his other grandmother gave it to him when he was born.

And from there, thoughts of motherhood jump, so that now on the kitchen table, I realize I might meet his biological mother someday if she ever looks for him, or if he seeks her out. In my heart, I can't bear to think he'd want another *mammina*, other than this one, his *carina*. And what if he really, really, really wants to meet her?

I concentrate on wiping my hands, and on baptizing and irrigating the mounting strips of peppers with a dash of balsamic vinegar. I may never meet her. I probably will never ever meet her. But what if? The thought insinuates itself so in my brain. Maybe I should tell her stuff about him—Nah! I begin writing an imaginary letter any-way, something like this: Dear bearer of my son at his birth—you see, of course, how I, master of avoidance, do not call her the word I can-not bear to share?

First, I must thank you for not aborting the wonderful gift you've lent me all these years—he's a delight, but you know that instinctively, you must though you haven't raised or seen him all these years. The skinny boy frame has changed, of that you're sure too, aren't you? But did you know he's almost 6'3" and has my eyes, my husband's love of sports and brain for business? And did you ever think that he'd be so deliciously sweet as to deliver kisses on my neck to interrupt me when I'm on the phone, making sure to get my full attention, or while I'm peeling peppers—kisses accompanied by tickles so I can't playful-ly slug him.

He's got your good looks, of that I'm sure, though we straightened his teeth; he's nearsighted, astigmatic, and been wearing contact lenses since he was fifteen. He's in college now—I miss him like the dickens so I write him cards and e-mails, and try not to call too much—don't want to break his you-know-whats allowing roomies to tease him.

He's home for Christmas now, and he loves red roasted peppers, the way his *abuela* made them, and I do. *Ay, querida Vieja,* dear old one, I have you in my heart and in my kitchen. Your beautiful grandson, has not forgotten you, nor will he ever, any season I make roasted peppers.

II

TONGUES

TONGUES

Wild with tongues of brushfire,
my reverie ignites a flame beneath the pasta pot.
I ring Signora Rosa Spina's bell across the hall,
and hand her through the door
a plate of *lingua* garnished with parsley and garlic.

She invites me in, waving a letter in her scratchy hand.
Seated in Rosa Spina's marble-floored living room,
I translate the letter, neither English nor Italian,
but in a foreign tongue we both understand
though we have never spoken.

As light obliquely pulses,
bolting quickly past panes of glass,
a serpent's fork of hiss and crackle,
I adjust the tongue of my sneaker,
re-lace mud-stiff green and red Gucci shoe ties.

Rosa Spina's cat licks a paw with a rose tongue
I know is sandpapery while rain-tongues pelt lime trees
outside *palazzo* windows on Via Prisciano
where Rosa Spina and I were once alive,
and spoke of loneliness in tongues.

SARDEGNA GHAZAL

I open a bottle of *Cannonau di Alghero* to let it breathe as dusk
steps a pace beyond penumbra; internal shipyard lights switch on.

Alone after a dinner of *malloreddus*, renowned *gnochetti sardi*,
I attend workers, propelled in green shirts, until midnight.

"*Hood-Fois*" labels are soaked, perspiration arching half moons
under arms, foreheads drip in time to buzzing sewing machines.

The wind works up courage to blow full force
into spinnakers—fruits of their labor.

Full blue regalia, mainsails, topsails,
and multinationals gather to practice skilled avoidance.

They skirt each other and the half-hidden rocks
of the treacherous, perfidious, unfathomable

Maddalena Archipelago in the Bonifacio Straits.
Beauteous saint and sinner straits,

complicated as navigators
and parlance—a *dialetto sardo* all their own.

And you, Nina, speaker of foreign tongue,
sip wine on the upper deck of a ravaged boat

to watch chronometer workers—
time passage, or vigil till he returns?

SAN FELICE CIRCEO:

HUNTERS & GATHERERS

the woods

the oil flask

the garlic

the cornhusks

the lake

the blood

the breeze

the basket

the calling

the musk

the nostrils

the smoke

the haunch

the wild fennel

the arbor

the arrow

the whistle

the mushrooms

the pit

the stones

the wall

the horn ladle

the figs

the footpath

the hourglass

the cork trees

the apricots

the pine nuts

the coals

the lanterns

the pheasant

the quiver

the matchstick

the twilight

the chasm

the dew

the pelt

the foot

the rabbit

the raisins

the stew

the fire

the cook pot

the olives

the waterfall

the stake

the gate

the nanny goat

the honey

the woodpile

the kindling

LAKE GEORGE

Is the girl haloed by light,
essence of moon,
or moon itself?

Is the boy with fish-
ing pole, catching a fish,
or is the fish strumming the boy?

Is the mother in the porch rocker
whistling to the baby,
or is it wind in slats?

When the Calamine Lotion
no longer stops the itch, will a helping
of Grandma's apple pie do the trick?

Have you always believed
in the dynamics of family fusion?
The indigo vase upon the mantle undulates,

or is it a figment of imagination?
Is the vase on the cracked mantle—
brimmed with cobalt,

or is undulation,
a dream of plenitude?
When did midsummer girls

become sunbathed women?
When did they begin to serve
strawberries and cream?

Do the ingredients of summer
days beckon us to lie on carpet-
less bewitched parquet?

Can the flooring, which to touch,
though pristine and cool,
possess true beauty?

The smell of freshly
mown grass, changeth
not our universe one iota.

IN SUMMER

it is the metronoming
of dusk
that sets my heart
quaking:
Lipari.

*

We summered
lather blue
tongue of the ocean
tongue of the moon sea
delicate
smooth
cool apparatus lick
& mist diamonding you
rose spray
pant or go.
No, not rose, freesia
profumo piccolissimo,
wee & lilliputian,
like milking a gecko.

*

We ate on a terrace over-look-
ing the sea
that gifted
us our *pranzo*
of grilled swordfish,
crisscrossed with prisoner's stripes,
bathed in Sicilian
lemon, irrigated *Corvo Salaparuta*
crowned by curly *prezzemelo,*
capperi, olive
served in *trattoria* light
invited by light as only light can be
on one of the Aeolie Islands.

LOVER OF BASKETS

Hampers, panniers, scuttles, buckets, creels, dossers,
punnets, and chip are some. She collects woven,
interlaced, zig-zag, braided, plaited, strung, twined,
twisted and coiled baskets made from branches, cord,

wicker, hemp, palm, jute, straw. They are painted, raucous,
riotous, varnished, natural or unvarnished, some decorated
or lined fleecy soft stuff or batting with overlaid calico;
others are bordered: fringe, ruche, furbelow, ruffles, ribbons,

tassels, flounce, frills, pleats. Summering in Circeo,
she removed two odd favorite flatter ones from decorative
place of honor adorning dining room walls—idiosyncratic
and supine, but baskets nevertheless—their 10 centimeter

high branched sides a twig-edged interweave, squared-off
north nose and south toes, bizarre Klondike snowshoes.
She used these semi-shoes to dry plum tomatoes sprinkled
with sea salt, roof-setting them to perspire and dehydrate,

sweat like her in sweltering sun, foreseeing a shriveling
perfection to *pomodori secchi* consistency in hot
Mediterranean sun. But it rained that year. Another year,
she exploited their flat and prostrate capabilities to scorch

abundant croppings of green and black figs. With soft
downy fig leaves, she lined the inside of a tote basket.
These *foglie* reminded her how she'd stuffed velvety lovelies
of the same quality the summer after a Greek Isles sojourn.

She plucked figs sugar-sweet from limbs, their honeyed
anuses dripping, a come hither bid to bees who overstayed.
She laughed, remembering her mother's words, *ospiti
e pesce dopo tre giorni puzzano* (invited guests and fish

stink after three days). *Mamma, dove sei adesso?*
She quarried these final fruits of summer, once even
invading a deserted neighbor yard, to gain access
to untended taboo trees. Fleeting thoughts of other gardens,

orchards, copses, groves, forests, thickets, woods,
farmlands, plantations, and coppices enraptured her.
She meandered among trees, in the gloaming of summer's
twilight and her own last sprouting sense of wild youth.

She filched, snatched and borrowed, minus the intention
to pay back. Ah! how she empathized with Eve,
Mother of all fruit pickers. Later, ever the Circeo gleaner,
she deflowered her baskets to split, quarter, and dry figs

above summer-slow smoke fires under a thatched lean-to,
almonds from Palermo tucked inside their bellies afterward
when they were skewered and shafted onto overgrown
opaque wooden picks, impaled upon mini-stakes.

When late *fighi settembrini* ceased to procreate, and only
spattered pulp remained as bird feed, the same flat baskets
were employed for *porcini* mushrooms garnered
from the forest floor. *Funghi* were dusted of bosk coats,

and skinned in spots. When she'd picked a *chilo*, minus
basket weight, she quit the thicket, headed home to slice,
dice, and dissect every floppy fat cap and chunky stem till
every white-villain-white worm,

cajoled by scorching sun, inched their tiny bodies out
in an undisciplined array of crawls, slithers and creeps,
squirming suicidally, to a concrete resting place below.
The following year in Porto Vecchio, Corsica, her husband,

disprezzando sempre, cajoling and saying what a waste
baskets were, purchased for her a woofed and bias-warped
market beauty, she couldn't bear to live without
to bear the fruits of summer.

Upon her return to Circeo, she filled this comely *cestino*
with chaplets for the chapel nearby the *panificio*.
On her way home, she bartered flowers for *pizzapane*
and hard biscotti to dunk into *vin santo* after supper.

Wending her way, she stopped at a market stall esteeming
the basket-maker's wares. One south Floridian morning,
she reaches for a crusty loaf to slice and toast. Her hand
caresses smooth wicker of years. Each basket stroke

rekindles memories of Corsican hillocks
and lanes her younger knees negotiated well,
and where her lover bargained for this basket
for his lover of baskets.

TONIGHT

Drydock living slips and rudders us into September days.
I spy sailmakers while I prepare an antipasto

of raw *ricci di mare*—sea urchins lemony and lush—
I sprinkle them with *Vermentino di Gallura*, then take a sip.

Such precision: the sea's bounty, my crisp wine,
sails measured on a warehouse floor.

Aft of my not too operable "yacht,"
I watch fish jump clear out of the water.

Water I have defiled with my soapy dishes.
Water replete with replica three quarter moon,

a lit lantern over *Porto Cervo Marina, Sardegna*.
Magic. *Magia.* I swear it.

I pity everyone who is anywhere else
but in this windless, cloudless Sardinian port tonight.

Black gypsy hair holds the North star;
the flood lights of the shipyard

reflect upon the water,
the 12 meter basin for sailboats.

I am docked beside an almost winner,
the "*Azzurra*" and know exactly how she feels.

I hail the moon, lift my frosted glass to cheer:
Cin-cin, l'chayim, a votre santé, down the hatch!

There is nothing I cannot feel,
Or do not know tonight.

THE BEACH AT ANZIO

Though not marine biologists,
we are gatherers
of Phylum Mollusca—
lumache di mare—sea-snails
& *padelle*—tiny upside down fry-pan
mollusks, soft unsegmented bodies
clinging to the quay rocks
beneath protective mantles
of calcareous shell.

You & I walk the shore,
scoop by handsful
leafy lettuce-like seaweed
to make fried squid fritters,
that'll sputter in hot oil,
a semblance of us
in our bubbling matrimony.

Your sigh—
warm & sweet,
anise-tinged—
the breath of God at dawn—
yet a cold gust
when your questions flay me
with your flogging tongue.

My scream—
jagged like the jetty—
as we dive into breakers
& stroke through cobalt
waters of the Tyrrhenian Sea
to a sandbar,
or snatch & stow sea urchins
in fishnet satchels
swimming behind from ankle ties.

Later we break apart
these spiked devils,
sprinkling on lemon & scooping
out insides with crusty *pizzapane*
or dip into a broth of razor
clams, mussels,
sea truffles with red tongues

like the red handle
& slash blade buried in sand.
Good, you say, for whittling
away individuality
into a whole indistinguishable
other composite, or, I say,
Perhaps our time together.

Marathon walkers,
on a topless beach,
we watch wind-sails careen,
wind-surfers careering
into each other
a mess of tangled boards,
sails & mild curses.

Lightning fractures
azure sea & sky blue
architect's paper, dazzling
your face brimming summer tempest.
Thunderheads, irate & mordant,
explode like fireworks;
we seek shelter in a fisherman's shack—
I'm always late to recognize
a squall or squabble.

Rain pelts your cheeks
& furrowed brow.
A lookout at the point,
a helmsman foundering at bay,
I set my compass
by your agony awash
& want to kiss your mouth
& touch your tanned cheek,
but you shake your head.

I find turquoise bits among shells
disgorged in a rage of sea.
These, I place into your hands,
remnant mosaics from Nero's castle
before he & I went wild
with last night's incendiary torches,
burning more
than Roman aqueducts & bridges,
by the look of you.

THE DEER SLAYER

It finished in beauty,
at his soul's choosing
not in the mist of hills obstructed
where one cannot see mountain peaks.
His house, fashioned of dawn,
held a river for eels and gulls, a forest of trees for eagles' nests.
His heart knew configurations of sorrowful branches falling
under heavy snow,
leaves thrashed by nomadic winds.
Also twilight.
His sense of clouds loomed dark at times,
at others, a transparency sketched by lightning darting
crooked alleys across the moon.

I have married in days of thunder only to keep blankets of fur,
pillows of feathers, a cord of wood
nearby to chase foreboding echoes in air.
High above, in places of ordinance and disdain,
have I feared to walk
even in the softest chewed doeskin of my ancestors.

Earth. Wind. Water. Fire.
His spirit soars above mountain summits.
But my father's feelings, thoughts, ashes,
and name have I sucked down with the oyster,
clenching a shard of his bone
between my teeth with the meat of the crab.

FROM HERE TO THERE & BACK AGAIN

A coconut palm frond fell
upon the teak deck.
I toted it to the side
of the house to lay with others
for the landscapers to retrieve,
the broom-like tendrils
sweeping along garden stones
and a worn path made by our hunter dog.

One little act rowed me on
high waves of remembrance
and once again I was a young girl
walking my dog in a Roman *piazza*,
having been transported on a boat
to moorings of mornings
when I'd meet the street sweeper
Vittorio with his twig brush, pushing,
gathering, and dumping fallen cones
from secular umbrella pines
spilling *pinoli*,
cigarette stubs, paper cups—
all matter of debris
into cans marked SPQR.

Sometimes I'd see him in *Castroni*—
the coffee bar on the corner,
ordering cappuccino
laced with Vecchia Romagna,
brandy so strong it could
"grab your drawers,"
or "rot your socks off,"
my brother used to say.

The earth, damp and black
alive from recent rain,
now basks in sun
that browns the palm branches,
cooks the compost heap,
decaying a collage
of wood chips, loam, grass,
flowers from the frangipani,
and the dog's fertilizing gift.

LYCHEE NUTS & POMEGRANATES

Snow sparkles—mica, isinglass—
upon white attic wainscotting
of houses built to last,
brick chimneys iron initialed.

All around squirrel chirrups
echo from horse-chestnut trees,
the lost meadow thrush
dartling in dormant hydrangea,

his "so-long" song flits along
with him into pines, scented,
poignant, as wind sloughing
through cones, needles, branches.

Crossing city streets, I skate
a labyrinth of ice-slicked sidewalks
of a Korean War January
when the specter bridge appears.

The frosty walk across
winters intensely as light fades.
I begin to menstruate
on the way to Belladonna's

Pharmacy, whose name means
beautiful lady, yet also dead-
ly nightshade. Who'd think bell
flowers, adorned with innocent

glossy berries, poisonous?
Who'd mistrust them?
Warm wet crotched in my undies,
cossets me as the tiny bell rings

when I open the door—a gush of warmth.
I fidget waiting for customers
to leave one by one, two by two.
I muster courage to ask

for sanitary napkins
absent from display cases
or storefront shelves.
My cheeks burn cold,

fear, like the smell of blood
if I move too fast,
emanates, shimmers
in overheated confines

of the drugstore.
Mr. Belladonna, smocked
in wainscot white, tweaks
his mustache—a wink to say,

Had to happen someday.
Afterward, backtracking home,
the taste of lychee lingers
on my tongue not yet defiled

with words like "chink" or "dago."
In Cantonese, I'd said, *Mh'goi*,
bowing to the queued laundryman's son
picking up my father's starched, Caucasian shirts.

Then in spring a pomegranate gift,
lush red rivulets in my hand's
hilly gullies, knowing an almond stare
could make me pregnant now.

CRUISING

I wanted to live so I drove
the highways, byways,
thoroughfares and streets.
Lavender dawn
sleeked to black tautness
like the string of an unseen archer's bow,
held with a notched arrow, ever ready, ever aimed.
Swoosh of feathers as the mind's arrow
releases, unleashed shot, a powerful pull of fifty-five pounds.
Hiss of arrow's kissing flight piercing the target's bull's eye,
my bare feet atingle in high grass wet with dew.

Is it Spring yet? Where comes this taste?
Baby's breath commingled with the talcum-scented snow?
Why does a hummingbird stray her nest as steel shadows
wrest it from my grasp? Mimosa's hair blows blond in tormented
wind ripples—Raffaello's *Primavera* dances garlanded
with a corona of interlaced flora—memento mori of stillness,
perfect yet alive in every graceful movement,
a symphony of shafted beams
coming toward me until a flashing red light
makes me cease and desist, not persist.
But does anyone proceed with caution?

III

FOOD FOR THOUGHT

FOOD FOR THOUGHT

I eat audiotapes like pastry.
Nay, I devour them.
Binge
like I do on *mini-bigné*
cream puffs when Lent is over,
or fried or baked *zeppole*
for the feast
of *San Giuseppe*
when no one is looking,
sneaking them into the heart of dark nights
while the household sleeps,
unfazed by my recklessness,
deep in the fathomless pit of dreams.

Inspirational, novels, self-help, how-tos,
short stories, poetry, biographies and histories—
so innocent an evil,
or is it?
Maybe I should be seeking help—
group therapy, a psychologist or psychiatrist?
I wonder, engorging my ears,
stuffing words into them,
gluttonous for more even
after swallowing what I'm hearing,
if there's
an Audiotapes Anonymous
in our area.

POETRY

inside:
the parchment ignites
with my desire
for tethered art
intraductal,
calligraphied & chiselled

lobular light
nights
irrefrangibly
the dark ghost of foreigners

Stockholm
yawns
dawnwards
isochronal
from the throes of midnight

outside:
snowflakes shadowfall
almondy & whipped
froth filling in *semla*
streetlamp seedy *ora*
opaque as cloudberries
washed down with Linie

poetry *stanza*
like this room

WO KEE'S, CHINATOWN

(AFTER JOHN ASHBURY)

Fans on the wall,
a three panel divider screen
       tin over copper
       shining rivals ... mother of pearl, jade, cornelian,
       chalcedony, quartz, onyx

          afternoon
      dim sum feasting
      harkens tastes
cha sui bao—steaming
      pork buns
on baked blue enamel plates
            hands
                 grasp in misinterpretation
kua zi (quick little fellows) in pigeon: chopsticks
empathizing immeasurably

     a rustic sluice of prawns,
          of vulnerable chicken feet

                 dramatic lighting
            teaware & red lacquer seals
              on a black tray

*precise depiction
Calligraphy

the hidden mind
inverts, invents
events
Xian & the clay soldiers

at attention
season
of film noir—
Zhou Yu's Train
tracery
throughout *
nostalgia

scroll
discerns
rice paper   rice sake
rice with clams in black bean sauce

MY FEET OUTSIDE THE SHEET

There's a ketch in the stretch of canal at the back of my house.
On summer mornings I wake to find my feet outside the sheet—
Beating rhythms to the wind in fittings for the ketch's sails
And the down-to-the-bone of me wants to run away.

My feet are ready, but a golden anklet anchors me for now
As surely as my son's feathery eyelash kisses my cheek.
Slowly summer passes, and the ketch with her riggings departs
With the wind, and I, my feet, we are still here.

I look out at the quilted water under a canopy of queen palms.
And know I face the autumn—my feet will want the warmth
Of covers. Yet each day in dawn light, my cold uncovered feet
Dangle off the bed freely to an inner rhythm all their own.

I awake startled by silence until my mind explodes with:
And who will help him draw and color Argentina and Brazil?
Who will serve the turkey dinner trimmed by family ties?
I am beginning to despair over winter's advent,

But sing an inner lyric and coerce my feet to dance,
To help me brave with braggadocio my problems
Neatly boxed by cadence and the marrowing out of me—
I am beginning to fret guitar and the ketch's return.

HERE IS TOMORROW

Wisps of clouds scudding
across a used-up inkpad of sky—
dawn will bloom too soon today—
time told by extinguished stars
who have snuffed their beacons
just when I needed their fireglow most;
but the interval allows me to open
this last bottle of wine
whose label reads Ecco Domani

Here is Tomorrow, yours forever.
I raise my chalice skyward and say, *Cin-cin.*
I'll brood no more on God's way, or life,
and wash the dried mascara
all away with the garden hose.
I turn my bathed face to where a parrot
rumbles up his feather engine
in a queen palm, shadowing
the latticed water of the canal.
Gazing in that direction
above the sway of fronds,
a catch like an unfinished sob imprisons my breath
for there in the day's chiaroscuro beginning

a last star consumes itself
for this eternal night,
like you, the light
going out of your eyes.

WWW.INTHEBONDS.COM

& like magic notice of stocks, mutual funds, futures,
& Wall Street pearls fly the friendly skies of cyberspace,
over the internet, not by snail mail, but to your web-site
or e-mail address written in lower case, so ee cummings chic.

You log-on, point the mouse & choose from the menu,
which used to mean veal *parmigiana, osso bucco,* or
pasta primavera, but now refers to encrypted upgrades,
that translate: buy lo & sell hi, puts & calls, short sales—
unless you're dealing with a negative cash flow
& the VP of Morgan Stanley faxes your VIP office,
tries to get you on the horn, but your secretary
forgot to put your calls on hold. She's out-to-lunch has PMS,
feels harassed, over-worked & under-paid.
Now your phone is ringing off the proverbial wall
but really off the desk & the receiver's in the cradle
& you're not picking up till you hear the VP's message
there's an NSF stamp on your check,

so you hit the speaker button & the best response
your downsized brain comes up with is: "It's an oasis out here,
a veritable jungle, & check's-in-the-mail ASAP."
Then you dodge his next bullet with a quick
spreadsheet question, or a left-base hackneyed
comment on the primaries such as: "It's the bomb."
Or "Don't you feel affirmative action should include second
generation Italo-Jewish-American post-menopausal women
in their fifties enrolled in an MFA program?"

Thinking outside the box, the VP says: "My biggest choice
today should be do I get a mocha or latte to go from Starbucks,
or how many Viagra can an overweight, SWM's quadruple
by-passed digital fiber-optic heart sustain in one go while on-line
trading, saving or printing, copying to disk, trashing
& deleting, never panicking if the recycle bin is overloaded,
a virus attacks, or a worm attaches itself—
who are these hackers anyway?"

Just then you spy the headline of *Wall Street Whispers*:
LAPD catches & grills hackers on hot-seat: "Why don't you
use your smarts for something worthwhile from the get-go?"
Hackers say, with quasi-Quasar laser sentimentality,
"Where's the challenge?"
LAPD retorts: "Is that your final answer?"

SORIANO NEL CIMINO

WITH CLEMENTE THAT SUNDAY PLAYING BRIDGE WITH MICE

We scavenged potatoes in a quasi-fallow field,
canopied by *uva fragola* clusters—wild strawberry grape

that yielded three liters of jam. The potatoes Clemente
whipped into a thick potage doused with holy water

from a font, sprinkled sea salt, *benedictus* and *hosannah*
shower from virgin olive oil gleaned from last year's harvest.

For zest, he yanked an onion, green shoot sprouting,
from a twisted braid hanging near Jesus's Sacred Heart,

thorns engirdled in trochal piercing—fat globs of blood
dripping. Impressed, not by gore but by image power's

ability to transport me to Brooklyn, three thousand miles
and thirty-three years distance from where I now stood

recalling *Nonna's* often-venerated icon upon her bedroom
wall; her gnarled fingers clasped prayerfully towards

the bleeding heart, "*Perché? Perché?*" Then as if she'd
received His word said, "*O, Dio mio,*" and never spoke

again. *La nonna* glided into a forever sleep. Later we
played bridge in the farmhouse overrun by tiny field mice

Clemente insisted needed shelter just as we did from the wet
cold. And when Clemente challenged me for underbidding,

I remembered Grandma stepping from a coma and the bed;
how she knew before her entreaty to the Sacred Heart

that Charlie Monte had died; she was angry no one told her.
We asked her was she sure, Of course, she'd seen him haloed

bright on a lighted tunnel's far side, waiting for her.
I washed and Clemente dried, save one platter hosting

mini-victuals, cut and diced to mouse perfection,
I set beneath the bridge table adjacent to the kitchen.

LUCKY LIFE

(FOR: GERALD STERN)

Lucky life isn't one long string of horrors;
there are moments of peace as I live in between blows.

Lucky I don't have to return to Visitation Academy
where I wore a saggy blue uniform and tan lisle stockings
with oxford lace-ups; where the halls, corridors and passage-
ways reeked with boiling tomato soup from the refectory,
day in, day out; where a reed-thin nun cracked me over
the knuckles with a ruler for losing my place in the second
grade reader—sometimes I still feel the sting
on my steak-red hand.

But each year, in meditations, in poetry and fiction, I do go
back to Bay Ridge, Brooklyn, and the cloister behind high
gray walls. I skip rope, play hopscotch and dodgeball,
and stick samara polyps on my nose. I play tag around
Grandma's birdbath circled by purple iris and pick Grandpa's
black figs near rambling pink and white tea roses tiptoeing
lackadaisically on the garage sidewall.

This year was a crisis and I knew it when I kissed my mother
for the last time before the funeral director closed her casket,
and another crisis when my brother Bud and I picked
up her ashes in a corded box wrapped with butcher paper—
my elegant, snazzy-dresser Mom, her luminous dark eyes,
her gleaming smile of perfect white teeth that made everyone
think she'd been a movie star, and that accompanied her
all her life, even down the conveyor belt into the furnace.

My dream is I'm caught standing in front of the congregation
of cloistered nuns because I've not eaten my dry cheese
sandwich and switched it for a chicken leg from a Mafia don's
daughter. Penguins we called the nuns—and every eighth
grade girl is dressed as one of them, the most angelic
of these, niece of a hitman. Suddenly it's my turn to recite
a memorized essay about the order of nuns my habit represents.
Reluctance makes me stutter through the first sentence
of my report; then I repeat it once again. I say it yet again,
knowing it's all a sham, standing in a baggy habit six sizes
too large for my skinny bones. I'll never make a nun, and then
when I see the prioress's massive bottom overflowing the chair,
somehow this confirms my decision. I begin to laugh, though
she doesn't find it funny even when I point to her rear spillage.

My dreams, my untethered dreams, up close, far away,
in rain, in snow, in dark, in memory, out in space,
moving yet still, are a cache of letters to my past.

Dear St. Michael the Archangel, crushing the serpent,
in the middle of the lake behind those cloistered walls,
what will you do for me this year? Will you tug my ear
to remind me of how I swore that our beloved
handicapped Sr. Therese was in a motorcycle accident
with Marlon Brando, and how she read movie magazines
nestled between the covers of her Divine Office?

Oh lucky life without nuns at Visitation for whom my Mom
did volunteer charity work—the reason I learned to cook
when I was eleven—and where I was chastised doubly,
once the day of the presentation, which didn't scar,
and once at the grate with Mother Superior telling my mother
of my reckless behavior. That cicatrix, that curve
of my mother's sigh dying away, I carry with me to this day.

Lucky life is like that. Lucky there's reparation in dreams,
and memory to return to, and lucky you can redeem yourself
in baptizing waters from the bathtub font or shower stall
of a fresh new day.

Lucky there's tidiness to wash away and renew.
Lucky for me, there exists the mechanics of cooking,
when my mind recalls minutely and I live vicariously
the past—moments that make me wince or cry, feel guilty
or want to re-live. And luckier still, I think fast and say,
when you enter the kitchen to catch me weeping, it's the onions,
or I've just nicked my finger with the knife.

Lucky life. Oh, lucky, lucky life.

IV

THE CRUCIFIXION

THE CRUCIFIXION OF GARLIC

From the potted soil,
the young bulbs,
whiter than bluing white
in the last rinse water,
are yanked loose from dirt
and strung in bunches
by their own long thongs,
(like plaited palms
the Sunday before Easter
Hallelujah! Hosanna!)
twisted into meter length braids,
Magdalene's hair, beard of Christ.
Hung Christlike, corpus dangling
on the cruciform—
stone wall of the terrace
off the kitchen that I called *veranda*—
where we took our summer meals,
(*spaghetti aglio e olio*
when we were *lira*-less)
hoping for a breeze.
The patio's perch,
above the oleander, lemon, and persimmon trees,
overlooked the spectacular view

of the next door apartment building's
gravel parking lot,
into which you spit the cherry stones
of our youth, wishing next year
to see a fruit tree burst forth in bloom.
Sometimes you'd challenge me
to a contest of distance.
I always managed to lose
by forfeit through laughter,
or crying out, No fair,
because I'd swallowed a pit.
Their sheaves:
crossed fibers
of Chinese rice paper;
Egyptian papyrus before process;
tissue paper in a Christmas box;
Communion wafers;
scrolls
set to fluttering
if my shoulder brushed past
stirring them up,
setting them down
on the desks of scribes and Pharisees
who transcribe upon them.
And among this rabbinate
rebels, but counted few
in numbers.
Afraid, they hid behind
their titles, beards
and talliths.

Their uses many: to ward off vampires, to heal warts,
to infuse into boiling water, to make tisane, to feed
to dogs to kill their fleas,
cure-all, elixir, panacea
to treat high blood pressure,
circulation, cholesterol, arthritis.
The day I nailed
a newly uncurled wreath
upon a wooden crossbar,
a murmur made me bend
near and cup my ear to hear,
Forgive her for she knows not what she does?

Yet with each sharp blow
my hammer echoed mantra
for the messianic
Superstar of herbs,
shepherd of loose cloves,
principle aromatic in the fisherman's favorite,
gatherer of prostitutes and thieves
with knock-out breath who stroll the Via Veneto,
an ancient healing balm when placed
upon blind eyes,
leprotic sores,
possibly a raiser of the dead
if eaten in quantity
on toasted *bruschetta*.
I strike again, one last spike
to secure this interweave
upon its rood.
In need of cloves to season summer lamb
or rub on rabbit,

I'd twirl one lumpy golfball round
'round to rent it free,
and watch pilotless parachutes
billow slowly groundward.
Snowflakes puffed out full of pride,
grown fat as pigeon flocks,
breasts held high, they hunt and peck
corn, sunflower and pumpkin seeds
tossed by hordes of tourists in Piazza Navona
or medieval Dubrovnick before the war.
The Roman ones decked out in togas,
or Essenes holding a piece of the shroud
to cover an anointed body laid to rest
in a tomb of hewn stone
somewhere in the Holy Land.

AVE MARIA

In dreams
your India ink
hair streaks white,
silvering
like fractured lights sparkling
in a sky electric—
a coppice
of sultry summer and storm,
like the underside of olive leaves
in Isola di Capo Rizzuto
where once on a windswept hill
I rode horseback,
and ate grapes redder than *amarene* cherries,
so sweet
their aftertaste almost bitter,
not unlike
memories of you.

V
CHAOS

OUT OF CHAOS

From the agora crush,
I step into a wheel of alleyways
centered by a brazier
roasting couscous.
A hub of men in flowing gowns
scoop with bent fingers
from the communal pot,
licking mustaches clean
with pink tongues.

Barefoot I enter a mosque
in a cloche of veiled women
with henna feet & palms.
Later I watch men smoke
a water pipe
& sip sweetened tea
from steaming glasses.
I buy blue & pearl beads
knotted of silk threads
from a vendor closing his stall.

A carillon chime
bestirs my mind
to skyfall in peaching spring
& daffodils surrounding the lake in Sabaudia.
Sand. Wild onion above beach dunes
overgrown, reedy with rosemary,
cork trees, denuded, stripped,
nuts falling from umbrella pines,
juniper-like in fall
dancing leaps into dandelions.

I have loved you
bewildered & strange
by the rounded heights of Torre Paola,
Saracen beach watchtower, and skiing
Passo Gardena, snow still falling,
as we sipped *la grolla dell'amicizia*
hot from spigots caramelized
with burnt sugar
beneath the Amentarola
speck & pickling imagination still;
under cottony moons and dragon clouds,
spotting porpoise in the Tyrennian Sea,
island nightfall on Ventotenne
ferragosto—

Tonight Orion's belt bristles bright.
Far away places traveled,
remote, unrhymable
surrender to your Cerrutti aftershave's
soft spice scent,
& I am a hazy aura
with the nearness of you.

Maps unravel
us, my cartographer,
standing slikspun still,
threading in & around ourselves
parabola arcing,
infants again
in mother's womb,
afloat in amniotic fluid,
caressed
a shield of life-sustaining fluids
rock & cushion.
His words, or mine?

I hunger for song, song, song.
Or a *shahada*.
Minaret bathed in sunlight
sparkles the munificence of Allah.

The muezzin calls the men to prayer.
Behind billows of hashish,
I glide the El Khalili souk;
accosted by hawkers,
I bargain away lipstick & mirrored case
for fine Egyptian cotton,
intimate weave, conjuror,
vicarious amulet keepsake,
& cover my head with the *hijab*.

IN MY HEART, IN MY BLOOD

A restaurant proprietor in Portland's Chinatown
says I smell sweet as I pay the bill,
so I confide that centuries ago my great, great, great
grandmother's grandmother brought scents with her
hitching a return ride from Old Cathay
with the famous grower of saffron, Marco Polo.
And to this day my relatives abound
in places like Trogir—even after it was part of Marco's
native Veneto nuzzled in the Adriatic Sea.

Then on a bet I travel to Turkey
just to see twilight swagger on the Bosporous,
to have my fortune read in coffee grounds,
indicating a flight to the Orient
just to taste giant prawns
drunk in *san hua* rice wine—
three flowers—invented 1000 years
before and still the fragrant herbs
are added and mixed to spring water
from Guilin's Li River near Elephant Hill.

Once again I'm on a train leaving Istanbul;
I sleep on the Orient Express,
smuggled *san hua* beneath my couchette,
dreams of me in a red silk cheongsam
holding hands with the restaurant owner
as musicians play the *pipa* and *yangqin*
in the park by the river,
and in time slower than slow motion,
we dance.

CHRYSANTHEMUM FIRE POT

In a red room with nine golden dragons,
we sit at a low green table.
At its center a copper bowl,
flame beneath its belly.
In shark broth,
floats one white chrysanthemum.
One-thousand year-old eggs
wobble on a plate near serving dishes
of prawns, carp, duck, spinach,
pig, squid, dried bean vermicelli.

Our Chinese cook shreds the flower—
its petals filament,
falling feathers from angels' wings,
into bubbling consommé,
One by one, he selects a morsel
to immerse and poach in the broth,
then dips it into frothy eggs and sauce.

Lastly we sup bean threads,
flavored by the rich soup,
this dense dollop on a spoon
lifted to our mouths,

mouths savoring the essence
of the predator of the sea,
graced and spangled chrysanthemum.
We gnaw the ocean's chiliad gifts,
never again to thirst or hunger,
tasting a thousand years—
love and loss.

ALL MANNER OF THINGS ... AND YOU

The manner in which the mourning dove hoots a three-note
   trill outside my window to wake me, and in that quasi-
   dream state, I listen to grasshoppers jump in the meadow.

The manner in which Scotch thistle, east of the Cascades,
   raise hairy heads—a field of praying mantis invoking
   sunshine, or wheat swaying to a chorus of angel chant.

The wind-lashed manner in which palm fronds thrash
   in a hurricane, the same way you move in sorrow.

The manner in which you're a sweet ripe fig one day or lonely
   as an empty room, but the sight of a newborn colt
   brings tears to your eyes always.

The manner in which we swim to the sandbar after the storm
   in San Felice; our feet seek holes in the sand, a razor
   clam beneath burrowing deep to escape our grasp.

The manner in which the air changes right before hail begins
   to blight a crop of melon—melons we'd have eaten
   with prosciutto.

The manner in which early each morning after rising
    and donning the tzitzit and the tallit, the same ten men
    walk to the synagogue on the corner, rain, sleet, snow
    or sunshine; they climb the steps holding down
    the rims of their black hats, and how I dare you to ask
    what they do after Shacharit, their morning prayers.

The manner in which the angels on the bridge that crosses
    the Tiber to Castel Sant'Angelo live and breathe
    in the swirling haze of autumn.

The manner in which in a nameless trattoria
    in Castelli Romani, the fire roars in the hearth,
    and, feeling the first chill of fall, we clink glasses,
    saying *cin-cin*, and I can't grab the camera fast
    enough as you lean over to kiss Marie, fall off the chair,
    sprawl head over keister, and laugh out loud.

The manner in which our hands scoop up jewels of tiny
    thumb-nail clams—topaz gold, peridot green,
    and amethyst violet on a Greek island in view
    of Skorpios, and later toss them with spaghetti
    when the moon hangs huge and round as the serving
    platter we eat from.

The manner in which a trout whirligigs on your line,
    and you say too bad the fish didn't swim faster,
    or hadn't been such a glutton.

The stealth and manner in which rabbits and birds approach,
    coming in from the desert at dusk to wait for seed
    we throw beneath the saguaros.

The sly manner in which you turn a knob and shower us
   with the hose as we lounge on deck chairs.

The manner in which my brother pictures me, riding horseback
   on mountain trails, or sitting on the veranda penning
   words in a leaf-bound journal, and in between the lines
   sipping wine from a long-stemmed crystal goblet
   you hand me—Bud's got the image right, right down
   to the Sassicaia, red as garnet in our mother's ring.

The manner in which the needle pricks my finger and blood
   oozes onto the white cotton sock I've never learned
   to darn, darn it.

The manner in which earth smells sweet after rain; and the path
   suctions our sneakers as we pop them free; looking back
   at Uncle Frank's country house from down the road,
   you tell me, how as a boy in Sicily, you delivered bread
   at dawn and by noon were too exhausted to eat.

The sweeping manner in which clouds outside my window
   form the hand of God, a different pose than in the Sistine
   Chapel, or yesterday before snow began to fall.

The pensive manner in which you put on sandals, then ask me
   to find keys already in your pocket.

The manner in which your gaze fixes on a body swan-diving
   off the trellis bridge.

The manner in which autumn gives place to winter and leaves
    furl and eddy, whisked away to the other side
    of the street, colorful as the child's duck-handled
    umbrella turned inside out with the wind.

The manner in which you smiled when I last saw you,
    and how the image remains painted, a still life in my brain.

The manner in which I turn around hearing you call me,
    Dad, though you're gone sixteen years.

ALONE IN GUILIN

At a traffic light
I gaze out the bus window
a man's scissors
snip black paper,
& my instant silhouette,
figure & profile,
appears miraculously—
an offering at 10 *yuan*.

My attention flags,
drawn to a screeching car
slamming a velocipede,
hurtling bicycle & rider
into an acrobatic flip
through cacophonic air,
landing on a hay truck.

Late morning as mauve mist
dissipates from Guilin air,
I eat *dim sum*,
'touching your heart,'
chicken feet, dumplings,
bowls of white rice,

& in the steam above
images of yesterday's fields & paddies
workers bent, arms pumping
like engine pistons
with the furor of their gleaning.

From a bamboo curtained window
of the restaurant,
I glance outside
where *yacamein* spills
from a workman's bowl
near smoke swirling
above a brazier of barbequed pork—
thoughts leap backwards
to breakfast: pork buns, black tea, *congee*—
when you reached across the table
to take my hands in yours,
so real the remembrance
of your touch, that startled,
I jump backwards,
a bike-less acrobat.

MEETING

Underneath streetlamps at dusk the city reflects
in rain-pooled cobbled streets, whose shine and verve
transport me to the riverport of Ostia where antique Roman

ballast stones from ships, line forgotten roads,
haphazard, rubicund and ruvid. I walk a little faster
on the less traversed Ghetto streets, especially near Teatro Marcello,

do I race, but time slows ... 46 B. C.
Julius Caesar ordered this construction
avanti cristo—before Christ, oh, sweet soul of Jesus, sanctify me.

You didn't meet me for *un gran caffè* this afternoon,
at the bar in Piazza Sant'Eustachio, so I sipped a lonely tea,
and nibbled on the apricot jam center of a bull's eye cookie.

Tonight, Christ and autumn's advent consecrates me
in a cleansing drizzle, at our appointed hour
by our favorite fountain in Piazza Mattei—

la Fontana delle Tartarughe—
the fountain of the turtles, but if truth be told,
the turtles were added later to Bernini's youths,

arms and hands upheld, upturned.
How joy springs from those lithe bodies.
And again, you didn't come to meet me.

Not for the afternoon coffee break,
nor for our usual encounter of nocturnal love.
It stopped raining, now underneath a pitiful half moon

and panoply of stars, I know
you'll never meet me here, or there,
or anywhere else ever again.

THE SHIRT

Not just a cotton blouse but the color of summer corn;
one hundred teensy cloth-covered
buttons Cossack fashion;
purchased at Macy's for $17.50
in 1967, the year we married.
My silver hair was shiny dark
back then and *ochi chyornye* eyes
held no corner wrinkles reading the Russians—
Tolstoy to be precise.

I rummage through our old leather
steamer trunk for that errant tunic,
then later on the Internet, search for former friends
and the only other quasi-serious beau—
I was just 16. His name was Alexei,
his mother, Tamara, taught ballet.
I imagine the twists my life
would've taken had I married
him—we drank vodka, ate caviar and blini
after a recital once—
instead of the guy who's held
sway over my heart for 39 years.

The only thing remote-
ly Russian about him
is he's a bit of a Gypsy—
a vagabond with means who loves to travel.
Last year we deposited a stone
on Dostoyevsky's grave
in Tikhvinsky Cemetery in St. Petersburg.
We visited the Haymarket, Sennaya Ploschad,
on the Metro stop of the same name
twixt the Fontanka and the Griboedova.

Or else from Kazan Cathedral,
we followed the Griboedova south or west—
away from Spilled Blood—
ten measly blocks to the market,
to be offered tastes
from a honey seller's stall;
now how I wish I had that yellow shirt
to stow again in my suitcase to wear
for day-dreams in a field of dandelions
near the Summer Palace or the Hermitage.

IN THE VALLEY: A MEMORY

Reader, I own a remembrance,
which cannot be placed.

It doesn't square, but rounds,
when I want it boxed.

How to catch it? Where to quarter?
I ask myself if it's a dream, a veil

lifted from a former life,
a piece of someone's history,

déjà vu, a fraction of a story,
imagined or real?

I'll draw it for you now,
please watch me sketch

as I chalk upon a slate
a country bungalow—

windows circle the porch,
a thatched roof inclines.

See its fringes?
Am I a kindergartener

dressed in plaid jumper?
Gazing out the window

toward rainbowed horizon,
no roads beckon—

not hither nor beyond; no carts
move, no horses neigh or whinny.

The cottage, high on hillock, floats on air,
nestled somewhere in primordial val,

lush, green, foresty—a fairy tale, yet not.
In the distance soft meadows spread,

the mournful caws of doves,
the lowing cows & an abundance

of light, light, light.
Warmed by afternoon sun,

a sleepy radiance
bathes the veranda,

& on wicker glass-topped tables
marshmallows melt in steaming cups

of chocolate & plates of sugar cookies
are dotted with one red hot cinnamon,

& where fat, round pastel chalks
to draw & scribble lie,

a regiment of odd-shaped soldiers,
on the ledge of a framed blackboard,

copper hinged on ashwood,
a ridge full of dusty erasers.

Do we speak in a language without words
to others who were there, but now are gone?

Springtime after rain everything glistens
sleek & shiny, birds fly over the glen.

I've seen it all, but where?
I'm lost in a memory.

FORM & THEORY

As I wait for pasta water to bubble & boil,
I smack my lips, thinking of Mamma's tomato sauce,
touching kitchen condiments she'll never use to scatter
in dishes to season anything ever again.
I salt the water, watch foam froth
in eddying swirls as I stir in *rigatoni*,
recalling her flavorful *rollatini*,
she always called *spedini*.

For years, I stood at her side embezzling
preparations, purloining secret
flips of the wrist to pound cutlets to paper thinness,
filching, for later use, the way she sliced away impertinent
gristle or sassy fat, plagiarizing how her hands dipped
into mixed breadcrumb she'd fling onto the meat,
then top with grated parmesan, forming tiny wells
so quickly I barely catch the precision timing
in her flicking finger, or drizzle of olive oil.
She tucks in edges, spins, wheels, rolls
rollatini into perfect bite-sized pieces
I've never mastered the art of making.

The theory of her form
transfigures, mutates, metamorphoses daily.
When my mother was still my mother,
her kitchen feats were renowned, but are now a reverie,
unfolding, like a backward walk up stairs.
Her sinewy hands, gnarled as ginger root,
no longer cook or cut, butter or bake, stew or steam,
but brush unseen crumbs from lips,
hands, ever more uncoordinated,
missing destination after destination in futile attempts.
Sometimes she pokes her eye, or by mistake her nose,
target of wrong intention.

I am my mother's child learning cooking lessons.
Here's one I haven't mastered—memories. I eat memories raw.
In form & theory I am my mother—every woman
is woman's child. Our world passes by in silent roar—
all our friends are dying, no one's left to call our names.
Every woman, Mom & I pass on.
Who in this world will remember?
We were every woman in our time.

AUTHOR'S BIO

Nina Romano earned a B.S. from Ithaca College, an M.A. from Adelphi University, and a B.A. in English and an M.F.A. in Creative Writing from Florida International University.

Before moving back to the States from Rome, Italy, where she lived for twenty years, her poetry appeared often in the newspaper *The Rome Daily American*.

In 2003 she read at the Miami Book Fair International, and at Books and Books.

Fall 2004 she co-taught a poetry and fiction workshop, "The Gastronomical You," with writer/editor Tracey Broussard at the Main Library in Fort Lauderdale.

Romano is an Adjunct English Professor at St. Thomas University, Miami Gardens, Florida.

PRIZES

In 2000 Romano received Honorable Mention for the Christopher F. Kelly Award for Poetry sponsored by the Academy of American Poets, judged by Catherine Bowman.

In 1997 she won First Place in the FIU Books & Books Graduate Poetry Prize for "The Crucifixion of Garlic," judged by Richard Tillinghast.

In 1994 Nina Romano won First Place for her story "A Kiss by the Greenhouse," in FIU's Josephine Friedman Undergraduate Fiction Award.

Printed in the United States
113543LV00002B/409-426/A